God's little book of Emotional Health

Elliot Msindo

Published in 2020 by the Stanborough Press Ltd., Alma Park Industrial Estate, Grantham, England.

British Library Cataloguing in Publication Data. A catalogue record for this book is available from the British Library.

ISBN: 978-1-78665-091-7

Scripture quotations are taken from the following versions:
English Standard Version – UK (ESVUK)
Good News Translation (GNT)
New Century Version (NCV)
New International Version – UK (NIVUK)
New King James Version (NKJV)
New Living Translation (NLT)
The Living Bible (TLB)
The Message (MSG)
The New Testament in Modern English by J. B. Phillips (JBP)

Designed by Abigail Murphy.
Printed in India.

Evidence of design

'The brain is more than an assemblage of autonomous modules, each crucial for a specific mental function. Every one of these functionally specialised areas must interact with dozens or hundreds of others, their total integration creating something like a vastly complicated orchestra with thousands of instruments, an orchestra that conducts itself, with an ever-changing score and repertoire.'
Oliver Sacks

'I praise you, for I am fearfully and
wonderfully made.
Wonderful are your works;
my soul knows it very well.'
(Psalm 139:14, ESVUK.)

Emotional health problems such as depression or anxiety are easily masked. Unlike physical ailments, we often do not see the pain that sufferers experience. Some will have difficulty even getting a diagnosis. No one – by ethnicity, social class, gender, age or even religion – is immune. There are many Christians who suffer from depression and anxiety who have a strong faith in God, but are not able to feel His presence due to their poor emotional health. For those of us who do not suffer in the same way, this is a hard reality to understand.

Within this miscellany of quotes and Bible verses is a collection of poems by Elliot Msindo entitled 'My Journey – My Fight'. The poems, heartfelt and intensely personal, discuss specifically the relationship between the individual suffering from mental health problems and the church community, seeking to invoke greater understanding between them.

' "My Journey – My Fight" looks at the personal struggles people suffering from mental illness go through. The journey refers to life on this earth as we live, and also to preparations for our journey to heaven. Stress, anxiety, depression, bipolar disorder and schizophrenia are some of the battles faced by people on a day-to-day basis. Life has become a journey and a fight for others, and these poems expose the struggles as well as the hope that everything we go through can be solved if we believe in God. It is difficult to understand mental illness if you have not suffered from it before, but if we take time to support those suffering, it will help us understand the seriousness of it.'

Elliot Msindo

'Some of the most comforting words in the universe are 'me too': that moment when you find out that your struggle is also someone else's struggle, that you're not alone, and that others have been down the same road.'

Author unknown

Uplift me

They see me walking;
they see me smiling,

Like diamond, eyes sparkling,
as the door of the church welcomes me.

Face glowing
but heart blowing.

Hymns and tunes
send me into the distant future,
as solace eludes me.

I am swallowed up in depression
and swimming in a pool of sadness.

My heart yearns for the sweet words,
'God is in control.'

Uplift me with sweet tunes:
'What a friend we have in Jesus.'

'O Lord, how long will you forget me?
Forever?
How long will you look the other way?
How long must I struggle with anguish
in my soul,
with sorrow in my heart every day? . . .
Turn and answer me, O Lord my God!
Restore the sparkle to my eyes,
or I will die. . . .
But I trust in your unfailing love.
I will rejoice because you have rescued me.
I will sing to the Lord
because he is good to me.'
(Psalm 13:1-3, 5, 6, NLT.)

My house is burning

They marvel,
Looking at how polished I am,
Smiling wide,
Singing loud – 'Amazing grace',
Putting up a good front:
But my house is burning.

House stashed with flammables – anxiety;
House loaded with explosives – stress;
One move and I explode:
A Christian in a burning house!

God, save me!

'Help, God – the bottom has
fallen out of my life!
Master, hear my cry for help!
Listen hard! Open your ears!
Listen to my cries for mercy. . . .
I pray to God – my life a prayer –
and wait for what he'll say and do.
My life's on the line before God, my Lord,
waiting and watching till morning. . . .
with God's arrival comes love,
with God's arrival comes
generous redemption.'
(Psalm 130:1, 2, 5-7, MSG.)

Anxiety – my daily bread

As dark moments take over
Hope is taken over as well,
Anxiety turning into daily bread
Instead of the living Word;
Despair creating a hollow
As cares of the world cloud this poor mind.

Like Judas, I wander away –
Betrayal, joblessness, divorce –
My cup is full,
Tears of sorrow always gathering like waters
of the Red Sea:
God is the only one who can dry the Red Sea.

Like Jacob, I will fight until I overcome;
Like David, I will face my Goliath;
Like Hannah, I will persist
Until sadness is booted out!

'Don't fret or worry. Instead of worrying, pray. Let petitions and praises shape your worries into prayers, letting God know your concerns. Before you know it, a sense of God's wholeness, everything coming together for good, will come and settle you down. It's wonderful what happens when Christ displaces worry at the center of your life.'
(Philippians 4:6, 7, MSG.)

The vulnerable

Can you see them, Lord,
The widows and widowers
Who are struggling to look after their
children?
Death has robbed them
Of their physical and mental health.
As they lay their heads on the pillow
Their minds start racing
From Cape to Cairo.

Can you see them, Lord,
The orphans and the ageing?
Anxiety is the music;
Loneliness is their best friend;
Tears are their juice.
Questions about the future
Dry their marrow –
Watch over them, Lord!

Can you see them, Lord,
The widows and widowers,
the orphans and the ageing?
A million questions dance in their minds
As they are welcomed every church day
By laughter from happy couples,
Happy families . . .
They are forced to retreat into their shells
like snails –
Watch over them, Lord!

God sees

'From heaven the LORD looks down
and sees all mankind;
from his dwelling-place he watches
all who live on earth –
he who forms the hearts of all,
who considers everything they do.'
(Psalm 33:13-15, NIVUK.)

Young soul

A young lost soul
Seeking redemption
From the chains of mental slavery –
Can God be the answer?
Haunting suicidal thoughts,
Fearing to follow the steps of Judas Iscariot.
Young and confused,
Crowded by negative forces – drugs,
Battling to free oneself
From the firm grip of mental torture:
Endless pain and ache to the burdened mind.
At 20 – tomorrow is further than
the North Pole.

Stumbling into church
May quench the thirsty soul.
The big void – spiritual void –
Quickly fills up with a mountain of hope.
The renewed feet run
To a spiritual well.

'Come, all you who are thirsty,
come to the waters;
and you who have no money,
come, buy and eat!
Come, buy wine and milk
without money and without cost.'
(Isaiah 55:1, NIVUK.)

God – the Antidote

Who has the courage
To journey through the wilderness
With the scorching sun, thorns and brambles?
Living through each day
Without hope for a sunny tomorrow,
Struggling with a tired mind,
Mind muddled with life's stresses?

Every church day is a day to look forward to
But it comes and passes
Yet stress comes and camps.
Depression walks with me side by side
To and from church.
Walking into the congregation
Introduces the body and steals the mind away;
This glowing face
Represents an extinguished heart.

It is the physical affecting the spiritual,
Sitting amongst worshippers
But not worshipping –
Moving lips
But not singing –
Nodding this stone-cold head
But not understanding.

Depression, stress, loneliness –
A package tied to a tired heart.
Can you see such people?
Can you hear their voices yelling?
Can you find an antidote?

God is the antidote.

*'You, God, are my God,
earnestly I seek you;
I thirst for you,
my whole being longs for you,
in a dry and parched land
where there is no water.'*

*'You will seek me and find me when you seek
me with all your heart.'*
(Psalm 63:1; Jeremiah 29:13, NIVUK.)

A fish dying in water

When life tosses you up down
With not-so-much-wanted glitches
Has the Holy Spirit been displaced
By an unknown spirit
Which has colonised my vulnerable mind?
When prayer turns into blabbering
Because of these permanent strangers –
Depression, anxiety and stress –
'Two are better than one.'
Where is a hand reaching out to me?
The fish is dying in water,
Sinking in church –
Reach out!

'Hear my cry, O God;
listen to my prayer.
From the ends of the earth I call to you,
I call as my heart grows faint;
lead me to the rock that is higher than I.
For you have been my refuge,
a strong tower against the foe.'
(Psalm 61:1-3, NIVUK.)

The bank

Where is the bank
To deposit sadness
And withdraw happiness?
To sign off cheques
And pay off this debt with schizophrenia;
To ask the bank teller,

'How much do I still owe?'

To check my balance
And see how much health
Stress left for me?
To make an appointment
And discuss my future?

The queue is long and winding.

'Happy are those who are helped
by the God of Jacob.
Their hope is in the LORD their God.
He made heaven and earth,
the sea and everything in it.
He remains loyal forever.
He does what is fair for those who have
been wronged.
He gives food to the hungry.
The LORD sets the prisoners free.
The LORD gives sight to the blind.
The LORD lifts up people who are in trouble.
The LORD loves those who do right.'
(Psalm 146:5-8, NCV.)

It's me

Yes, it's me!
Every weekend morning
I tiptoe into church
And position myself right at the back
With the hope of sipping
From the everlasting well.

Yes, it's me,
Hardly visible but physically present,
Drowned in this pool of believers.
They exchange pleasantries
as I cuddle myself at the back.
I sneak out quietly – no one even notices.

Yes, it's me
With my heavy luggage.
I go back to my lonely life
Accompanied by my close friends –
Depression, stress and anxiety,
Crying myself to bed –
I wait for another Sabbath.

'Turn to me and have mercy,
for I am alone and in deep distress.
My problems go from bad to worse.
Oh, save me from them all!
Feel my pain and see my trouble.
Forgive all my sins. . . .
May integrity and honesty protect me,
for I put my hope in you.'
(Psalm 25:16-18, 21, NLT.)

Depression

A depressed mind
Never easily responds
To the sweet message,
'Cast all your cares on Him'
From the preacher
When no one cares to know
The causes of this depression.

A depressed mind
Never easily responds
To the sweet song,
'Burdens are lifted at Calvary'
From the choir
When no one is willing
To offer a shoulder to cry on.

Who is willing to help?
Meeting basic needs like Tabitha –
Is the church immune to mental illness?

'I am feeble and crushed;
I groan because of the tumult
of my heart. . . .
My heart throbs; my strength fails me,
and the light of my eyes –
it also has gone from me.
My friends and companions stand aloof
from my plague,
and my nearest kin stand far off. . . .
But for you, O LORD, do I wait;
it is you, O Lord my God, who will answer. . . .
Do not forsake me, O LORD!
O my God, be not far from me!'
(Psalm 38:8, 10, 11, 15, 21, ESVUK.)

The church

The church is there to love;
The church is there to cuddle;
The church is there to support;
The church is there to strengthen;
The church is there to reach out;
The church is there to comfort;
The church is there to protect;
The church is there to uplift;
The church is there to motivate;
The church is there to console;
The church is there to unite;
The church is there to say, 'You can'
When the world says, 'You can't';
The church is there to be everything to
everyone
As Jesus was all to all.

'Bear one another's burdens, and so fulfil the law of Christ. . . . So then, as we have opportunity, let us do good to everyone, and especially to those who are of the household of faith.'

'A new commandment I give to you, that you love one another: just as I have loved you, you also are to love one another. By this all people will know that you are my disciples, if you have love for one another.'
(Galatians 6:2, 10; John 13:34, 35, ESVUK.)

The only hope

As the sun sets
Hope flies away like a bird;
My head throbbing like a drum
I curl myself in the corner
Holding tight to the Bible – my only hope –
Trying to squeeze hope out of it.

Suffering from emotional pain
– but Peter also did;
Suffering from physical pain
– but Jesus also did;
Suffering from distress
– but David also did;
They give a glimmer of hope.

'But the LORD watches over those
who fear him,
those who rely on his unfailing love. . . .
We put our hope in the LORD.
He is our help and our shield.
In him our hearts rejoice,
for we trust in his holy name.
Let your unfailing love surround us, LORD,
for our hope is in you alone.'
(Psalm 33:18, 20-22, NLT.)

Redeemed

When deeply sunk,
Engulfed in flames of anxiety,
Swimming in a pool of stress,
Shouting for help
With a voice drowned by sorrows,
Surrounded by marauding lions
Baying for this boiling blood. . . .

Eyes transfixed
On the cross,
Singing, 'Redeemed by the blood . . .'
Calmness and peace ushered in:
Though poor materially,
Spiritual jar is filling up.

'My tears have been my food
day and night,
while they say to me all the day long,
"Where is your God?" . . .
Why are you cast down, O my soul,
and why are you in turmoil within me?
Hope in God; for I shall again praise him,
my salvation and my God.
(Psalm 42:3, 5, 6, ESVUK.)

Save me

I am scared;
I am terrified;
I am anxious –
Save me!

My life – as empty as a jar;
Only 20 but looking 50.
Life has wrinkled my health –
Save me!

Trapped in stress,
Life is now sour grapes.
Is death the solution?
Save me!

Mind always racing
Between lacking and loneliness,
Watching as my house is burning –
Save me!

I am depressed;
I am stressed;
I am panicking –
Lord Jesus – save me!

' "LORD, help!" ' they cried in their trouble,
and he saved them from their distress.
He calmed the storm to a whisper
and stilled the waves.
What a blessing was that stillness
as he brought them safely into harbor!'
(Psalm 107:28-30, NLT.)

Peace

Standing aloof,
Hands planted on the waist,
In a lounge cluttered
And scattered with broken pieces,
Watching blood-stained walls,
Watching this explosive present character –
Volcanic emotions erupting unannounced,
Sudden happiness turning into frustrations.

Blood silently dripping,
A result of punching the wall
For sins it did not commit;
But unfortunately unable to punch these
problems away:
Bottled anger – venting it on everyone nearby.

Pursuing happiness
But never catching up with it.
They say God gives peace –
Will I still be in one piece
By the time He comes?

Introduce me to Him
Before this rocking ship sinks.

'And he awoke and rebuked the wind and said to the sea, "Peace! Be still!" And the wind ceased, and there was a great calm.'

'Peace I leave with you; my peace I give to you. Not as the world gives do I give to you. Let not your hearts be troubled, neither let them be afraid.'
(Mark 4:39; John 14:27, ESVUK.)

Melodious hymns

Sing me
The melodious hymns
When, like a bomb, my mood explodes.

Sing me
The melodious hymns
When sadness camps in my heart
like a nomad.

Sing me
The melodious hymns –
Shoots up like a rocket!

Sing me
The melodious hymns
When I plunge into a pool of depression.

Sing me
The melodious hymns
When thoughts of self-harm
Bulldoze into my mind.

Yes! Sing them – the melodious hymns.

'The LORD *your God is in your midst,*
a mighty one who will save;
he will rejoice over you with gladness;
he will quiet you by his love;
he will exult over you with loud singing.'
(Zephaniah 3:17, ESVUK.)

Where is the church?

Where is the church
As the world groans,
Moans and wriggles?
Stress, anxiety, depression,
Bipolar disorder –
Who can let it know
That Jesus can cure?
Where is the church
As the world cries,
Running to and fro,
Seeking solutions
Hidden in our pockets?
Where is the church?
Where are the believers?

'Love from the center of who you are; don't fake it. Run for dear life from evil; hold on for dear life to good. Be good friends who love deeply; practice playing second fiddle.

'Don't burn out; keep yourselves fueled and aflame. Be alert servants of the Master, cheerfully expectant. Don't quit in hard times; pray all the harder. Help needy Christians; be inventive in hospitality.

'Bless your enemies; no cursing under your breath. Laugh with your happy friends when they're happy; share tears when they're down. Get along with each other; don't be stuck-up. Make friends with nobodies; don't be the great somebody.'
(Romans 12:9-16, MSG.)

I didn't mean to

When I shouted at you,
My voice booming the ceiling,
Rattling your scared heart –
I didn't mean to.

When I kicked, punched and screamed,
Using furniture as projectiles,
Spitting at you like a llama –
I didn't mean to.

When I went up and down
Ignoring you for days and even weeks,
Spending days cuddling myself in bed –
I didn't mean to.

I hope you will understand
Because I just can't help it.
Forgive and pray for me –
Because I didn't mean to.

'Look at me and help me!
I'm all alone and in big trouble.
My heart and kidneys are fighting each other;
Call a truce to this civil war. . . .
Keep watch over me and
keep me out of trouble;
Don't let me down when I run to you.
Use all your skill to put me together;
I wait to see your finished product.'
(Psalm 25:16, 17, 20, 21, MSG.)

A Healer

They describe You as a Healer –
Heal my tattered spirit.

They say You are a Mender –
Can You mend this anxiety?

One said You are a Cleaner –
How about cleaning my polluted spirit?

Can You take charge of a broken life?
Come and take over my mental well-being.

I heard You can control thoughts
and actions –
Would You mind chucking
suicidal thoughts away?

Someone preached that
You are Michael, a Fighter –
Can You wrestle this schizophrenia?

Do You really give calmness and inner peace?
Come in and calm these raging storms.

'When the righteous cry for help,
the LORD hears
and delivers them out of all their troubles.
The LORD is near to the broken-hearted
and saves the crushed in spirit.
Many are the afflictions of the righteous,
but the LORD delivers him out of them all.'

'He heals the broken-hearted
and binds up their wounds.'
(Psalms 34:17-19; 147:3, ESVUK.)

Living in isolation

As the wind blows
It blows away the little hope,
Hope as thin as a thread –
Can you hang in there for years?
Scared by imaginary things,
Sitting still but spinning around –
It's not worth it.
Living through continuous pain
For days, for weeks, for years –
Pain which is invisible
And oftentimes labelled madness –
Being as isolated as an island,
Anywhere outdoors,
It's a scary place.
Anyone outside my circle
Is a scary monster.

I need divine intervention.

'Listen to my prayer, O God,
do not ignore my plea;
hear me and answer me.
My thoughts trouble me
and I am distraught . . .
My heart is in anguish within me;
the terrors of death have fallen on me.
Fear and trembling have beset me;
horror has overwhelmed me.
I said, "Oh, that I had the wings of a dove!
I would fly away and be at rest." '
(Psalm 55:1, 2, 4-6, NIVUK.)

Ailing world

Sending the precious message
Of love, grace and hope
To an ailing world:

A world bashed and banged
Upon the hard surface of stress,
A world rattled by commotion –

Everyone losing something, health-wise,
Physical or mental –
Where is the answer?

Every professional field
– All run back and forth
Looking for answers;
Everything and everyone being tried
Except God.

' "Why spend your money on food that does
not give you strength?
Why pay for food that does you no good?
Listen to me, and you will eat what is good.
You will enjoy the finest food.

"Come to me with your ears wide open.
Listen, and you will find life.
I will make an everlasting covenant with you.
I will give you all the unfailing love
I promised to David." . . .
Seek the LORD while you can find him.
Call on him now while he is near.'
(Isaiah 55:2, 3, 6, NLT.)

Prayer for an orphan

The ever present pain
Of losing loved ones,
Pain serving as a reminder
That you are an orphan,
Bible clutched to the chest
As if it's a plant
Being watered by these tears –
The croaky voice,
Singing the last bit of
'What a friend we have in Jesus',
Sends the orphan to bed
Every night.

No one cares.
Remember this orphan, O Lord!

'Arise, Lord! Lift up your hand, O God.
Do not forget the helpless. . . .
But you, God, see the trouble of the afflicted;
you consider their grief and take it in hand.
The victims commit themselves to you;
you are the helper of the fatherless.'
(Psalm 10:12, 14, NIVUK.)

You are the answer

Lord, the world is straining;
Your people seek answers
To the world's problems.
People are burdened –
Their hearts ache;
Their minds crumble
With stresses and worries.
Their faith is waning
As their needs swell –

You are the answer, Lord.

'Come to me, all of you who are tired and
have heavy loads, and I will give you rest.
Accept my teachings and learn from me,
because I am gentle and humble in spirit,
and you will find rest for your lives.
The burden that I ask you to accept is easy;
the load I give you to carry is light.'
(Matthew 11:28-30, NCV.)

Heroes

Can you see the world struggling
Under the firm grip
Of fear, anxiety, stress, and depression?

Where is Judas
To tell the world that suicide
Is never an answer?

Where are Joshua and Caleb
To tell the world
To face its fears,
Even if it appears almost impossible?

Where is Jonah
To tell the world that
Running away and hiding
Is never an answer
But a problem?

Where is Tabitha
To tell the world that
The Gospel is not preached in the pulpit only,
But in the community as well?

Where is Joseph
To tell the world that
Life may take you through betrayal,
Prison and palace,
But faith and hope should remain firm?

The world is struggling.

'So do not throw away this confident trust in the Lord. Remember the great reward it brings you! Patient endurance is what you need now, so that you will continue to do God's will. Then you will receive all that he has promised.
"For in just a little while,
the Coming One will come and not delay.
And my righteous ones will live by faith.
But I will take no pleasure in
anyone who turns away."
But we are not like those who turn away from God to their own destruction. We are the faithful ones, whose souls will be saved.'
(Hebrews 10:35-39, NLT.)

Single

I remember the good old days,
The time when everybody stays
Shaking and laughing
From cheek to cheek, smiling;
The pastor pulling off his glasses,
Asking about our Sabbath school classes.

I used to narrate to the pastor
More like a commentator –
As I grew up
Isolation crept into my cup:
They all got married.
I remained.

I used to sit at the front
Late 20s, I shifted to the middle.
After that, I went to the back
Finally I am now out of the church.
I see happy families – kids;
For me the story is different.

No husband,
No child – it kills me.

'If the LORD had not been my help,
my soul would soon have lived
in the land of silence.
When I thought, "My foot slips",
your steadfast love, O LORD, held me up.
When the cares of my heart are many,
your consolations cheer my soul.'
(Psalm 94:17-19, ESVUK.)

God

Going downhill – life meaningless,
Engaging less and less,
Darkness expanding as light dwindled,
Anxiety unbridled:
A train derailing
With me inside – ailing,
Living under the influence
In the tiny circumference –
Mental well-being crippled,
Health debilitated.

Then came along a man,
A diagnostician:
The story has a happy ending.
He was able to reframe –
Is he not God?

'Do not hide your face from your servant;
answer me quickly, for I am in trouble.
Come near and rescue me;
deliver me because of my foes. . . .
But as for me, afflicted and in pain –
may your salvation, God, protect me.
I will praise God's name in song
and glorify him with thanksgiving. . . .
The poor will see and be glad –
you who seek God, may your hearts live!'
(Psalm 69:17, 18, 29, 30, 32, NIVUK.)

The way

I used to run
And run to seek refuge;
Voices following me
And blinding my mind,
Never giving me a break
To listen to the ache
Tormenting me
And burning my walls down:
Voices buzzing like a swarm of bees,
Voices coming from an invisible place,
Shepherding me into dark places,
Never into the light.

'Am I better off dead?'

A question accompanied by the voices
Stuck in my mind like glue.
I knew no other way
Until I found the Way –
God wrestled my soul
From the jaws of the devil.

'I lift my hands to you in prayer.
I thirst for you as parched land
thirsts for rain.
Come quickly, LORD, and answer me,
for my depression deepens.
Don't turn away from me,
or I will die.
Let me hear of your unfailing love each
morning,
for I am trusting you.
Show me where to walk,
for I give myself to you.'
(Psalm 143:6-8, NLT.)

Looking upwards

Wandering alone
In deep darkness,
Not knowing darkness
Until the light shines.

Carrying too heavy a load
When burdens can be dumped
At the feet of one who cares,
Suffering when not meant to.

Load is heavy
When looking downwards;
Relief comes
After you look upwards.

'The LORD upholds all who fall
and lifts up all who are bowed down.
The eyes of all look to you,
and you give them their food
at the proper time.
You open your hand
and satisfy the desires of every living thing.
The LORD is righteous in all his ways
and faithful in all he does.
The LORD is near to all who call on him,
to all who call on him in truth.
He fulfils the desires of those who fear him;
he hears their cry and saves them.'
(Psalm 145:14-19, NIVUK.)

When God seems silent

What can you do
when life heckles you –

Jeers you,
Mocks you,
And spites you?

Stress piling up like dirty laundry
When God seems silent
After bruised knees
Pleading with Him
To fight your battles,
Voices humming in your head
Like an organised choir,
Panic attacks multiplying
Like an organised choir,
Panic attacks multiplying
Like mosquitoes in summer,
Anxiety escalating
Like veld fire in a dry season.

What can I do
When God seems silent?

'Hear me as I pray, O LORD.
Be merciful and answer me!
My heart has heard you say,
"Come and talk with me."
And my heart responds,
"LORD, I am coming." . . .
Don't leave me now; don't abandon me,
O God of my salvation!
Even if my father and mother abandon me,
the LORD will hold me close. . . .
Wait patiently for the LORD.
Be brave and courageous.
Yes, wait patiently for the LORD.'
(Psalm 27:7-10, 14, NLT.)

Legion

Looking at the scars,
Involuntary bruises,
Tattooed all over this tired body
Is a reminder
Of the tortured Legion,
Isolated and abandoned
From the living
And herded by unknown spirits
Among graves.
This house – slowly turning into a graveyard.

No visitor;
No friend:

The four walls – splattered with blood
Oozing from this dry body.

It came to a halt
When someone stepped in.
Sanity has returned,
Just like Legion.

'The LORD is my shepherd; I shall not want.
He makes me lie down in green pastures.
He leads me beside still waters.
He restores my soul.
He leads me in paths of righteousness
for his name's sake.
Even though I walk through the valley of the shadow of death,
I will fear no evil,
for you are with me;
your rod and your staff,
they comfort me.'
(Psalm 23:1-4, ESVUK.)

Lonely man

Story of a lonely man
Singing joyous songs
Petitioning God – a thousand times
Seeking redemption
From the shackles of depression
Which has made itself permanent
Since time immemorial:
Depression hatching,
Panic attacks, anxiety and stress
Crippling every faculty
Of his once-blossoming life.
It happens –
When God seems silent.

'LORD, you are the God who saves me;
day and night I cry out to you.
May my prayer come before you;
turn your ear to my cry.
I am overwhelmed with troubles. . . .
I call to you, LORD, every day;
I spread out my hands to you. . . .
But I cry to you for help, LORD;
in the morning my prayer comes before you.'
(Psalm 88:1-3, 9, 13, NIVUK.)

A safe haven

Love and kindness
Can drive away sadness.

Every person who walks in through the door
Should not be left lonely by the door.

The church should be welcoming –
Otherwise, why stay when I am not welcome?

Some of life's burdens . . .
With a smile they are lessened.

A smile costs nothing,
But when shared it changes something.

A church should be a safe haven
Leading people towards heaven.

'Be agreeable, be sympathetic, be loving, be compassionate, be humble. That goes for all of you, no exceptions. No retaliation. No sharp-tongued sarcasm. Instead, bless – that's your job, to bless. You'll be a blessing and also get a blessing.'
(1 Peter 3:8, 9, MSG.)

No more

No more shedding tears
Day and night.

No more living a life of misery,
Torment and sadness.

No more confining myself
Indoors for years.

No more singing sorrowful songs
Covered in filthy clothes.

No more giving in
To stress, isolation and anxiety.

No more pretending
That I am fine when I am not.

No more chasing away company
When I surely need it.

No more listening to the
'You can't' voices,
Because God said I can.

*'For I can do everything through Christ,
who gives me strength.'*

*'Jesus told them . . . "I tell you the truth,
if you had faith even as small as a mustard
seed, you could say to this mountain, 'Move
from here to there,' and it would move.
Nothing would be impossible." '*
(Philippians 4:13; Matthew 17:20, NLT.)

What some do

As challenges escalate
Some struggle to cope
While some struggle to understand;
Some sit in church
Moving their lips while their lives are
crumbling down.

As problems multiply
Some retreat into their shells
Like tortoises
Because they feel as if God has abandoned
them.
Some look at them
And wonder why
Because they are not in their shoes.

As stress levels rise
Some give up
And opt for the unthinkable
Because of limited options.
Some look at them
Struggling without help –
After suicide, they start wondering why.

Where is the support
When it's needed?

'The human body has many parts, but the many parts make up one whole body. So it is with the body of Christ. . . . In fact, some parts of the body that seem weakest and least important are actually the most necessary. . . . This makes for harmony among the members, so that all the members care for each other. If one part suffers, all the parts suffer with it, and if one part is honored, all the parts are glad.
(1 Corinthians 12:12, 22, 25, 26, NLT.)

Give me hope

Give me hope,
Hope bigger than a mountain;
Give me calmness
In the midst of fears.
Show Your presence
When I am caught up
In stormy weather.

Give me hope;
Calm my anxieties
When I become hopeless.
Show me hope
When, like Thomas, I doubt –
Blow away the doubt.

'Yet this I call to mind
and therefore I have hope:
Because of the LORD's great love
we are not consumed,
for his compassions never fail.
They are new every morning;
great is your faithfulness.
I say to myself, "The LORD is my portion;
therefore I will wait for him."
The LORD is good to those
whose hope is in him,
to the one who seeks him;
it is good to wait quietly
for the salvation of the LORD.'
(Lamentations 3:21-26, NIVUK.)

Show me the light

Show me the light
When darkness overshadows me
In broad daylight;
When I see a dead end
While You see a bright end;
When I see no value in myself.

When I see stress, You see strength;
When I see depression,
You see progression;
When death seems to be the only way,
You say, 'No way' –
When I feel overwhelmed by burdens,
You say, 'I will carry them for you.'

'I am the light of the world. If you follow me, you won't have to walk in darkness, because you will have the light that leads to life.'

'For God, who said, "Let there be light in the darkness," has made this light shine in our hearts so we could know the glory of God that is seen in the face of Jesus Christ.'
(John 8:12; 2 Corinthians 4:6, NLT.)

Sunset

When the sun sets
And hope deserts,
Flying out through the window
As if to seek freedom,
The desire to keep friends
But finding oneself lonely
Because of throwing tantrums
And smiling the very next minute –
Who can stand that?
Bright sunshine
Then instantly, a ravaging storm.

Husband deserted
Children adopted
Friends vanished
Sadly isolated:
God, where are You?

'Hear me, LORD, when I call to you!
Be merciful and answer me!
When you said, "Come worship me,"
I answered, "I will come, LORD."
Don't hide yourself from me! . . .
You have been my help;
don't leave me, don't abandon me,
O God, my savior.
My father and mother may abandon me,
but the LORD will take care of me. . . .
I know that I will live to see
the LORD's goodness in this present life. . . .
Have faith, do not despair.
Trust in the LORD.'
(Psalm 27:7-10, 13, 14, GNT.)

Stormy weather

Sunshine brightens the day
After stormy weather:

A visit from a friend
Brings happiness
After weeks of loneliness.

A joke lightens the mood
After days of tenseness.

A smile brings joy
After years of isolation.

Songs of salvation bring hope
After a life of hopelessness.

'I waited patiently for the LORD to help me,
and he turned to me and heard my cry.
He lifted me out of the pit of despair,
out of the mud and the mire.
He set my feet on solid ground
and steadied me as I walked along.
He has given me a new song to sing,
a hymn of praise to our God.'
(Psalm 40:1-3, NLT.)

Having someone

Burdens become light
When you have someone to share with;

A meal is tasty
When you have someone to share with;

A journey becomes short
When you have someone to walk with;

Smiling becomes worthwhile
When you have someone to smile at;

Life becomes meaningful
When you have someone to live for;

A church becomes a family
When members care for each other.

'It's better to have a partner than go it alone.
Share the work, share the wealth.
And if one falls down, the other helps,
But if there's no one to help, tough!
Two in a bed warm each other.
Alone, you shiver all night.
By yourself you're unprotected.
With a friend you can face the worst.'

'You are my friends. . . .' (Jesus)
(Ecclesiastes 4:9-12; John 15:14, MSG.)

Food – my enemy

I look at people eating
And I can't stop marvelling –
I remember the good old days,
Yes – as a kid,
Potluck at church –
I was the first
To organise chairs and tables;
Yes – I couldn't wait:
That was back then.

I can't stand people eating;
I can't stand food.
The thought of rattling my rib cage
Because of uncontrollable vomiting –
What is wrong with me?
Locking myself up,
Never answering when food knocks;
Never casting an eye
When food walks in.

'Oh, God, my Lord, step in;
work a miracle for me – you can do it!
Get me out of here – your love is so great! –
I'm at the end of my rope, my life in ruins.
I'm fading away to nothing, passing away,
my youth gone, old before my time.
I'm weak from hunger and
can hardly stand up,
my body a rack of skin and bones. . . .
Help me, oh help me, God, my God,
save me through your wonderful love.'
(Psalm 109:21-24, 26, MSG.)

My battle

It is not a joke
But a battle,
Breaking down amongst congregants
For no apparent reason –
At least to them.
Every sermon
Being a message meant for me,
Hoping for a better tomorrow –
But how about today?

'We are pressed on every side by troubles, but we are not crushed. We are perplexed, but not driven to despair. We are hunted down, but never abandoned by God. We get knocked down, but we are not destroyed. . . . 'That is why we never give up. Though our bodies are dying, our spirits are being renewed every day. For our present troubles are small and won't last very long. Yet they produce for us a glory that vastly outweighs them and will last forever! So we don't look at the troubles we can see now; rather, we fix our gaze on things that cannot be seen. For the things we see now will soon be gone, but the things we cannot see will last forever.'

(2 Corinthians 4:8, 9, 16-18, NLT.)

Fear

Who can help me overcome?
Overcome this deep fear –
Fear engulfing me like fire,
Fire suffocating my breathing,
Breathing that has been a struggle,
A struggle because of health complications,
Complications that have crippled my life,
Life full of stubs and thorns,
Thorns pricking my sorry heart,
Heart swimming in a pool of fear,
Fear which has left me confined,
Confined in this miserable situation,
Situation making me live in an all-time low:
Low mood, low self-esteem, low motivation,
Motivation to seek help,
Help from this psychological trauma,
Trauma that has taken away prayer:
Prayer – the only tool,
Tool to pull me through.

'But when I am afraid, I will put my confidence in you. Yes, I will trust the promises of God. And since I am trusting him, what can mere man do to me?'

'Yes, be bold and strong! Banish fear and doubt! For remember, the Lord your God is with you wherever you go.'
(Psalm 56:3, 4; Joshua 1:9, TLB.)

The future

Looking back
Over my shoulder,
Watching dust
Covering my hazy past,
Rendering it invisible:
Battles buried,
Addictions tackled,
Challenges whipped –
A true testimony
Of divine intervention;
Starting on a clean slate
I march on:
The past is for experience
But the future is for corrections.

' "For I know the plans I have for you," says the LORD. "They are plans for good and not for disaster, to give you a future and a hope." '

'I focus on this one thing: Forgetting the past and looking forward to what lies ahead, I press on to reach the end of the race and receive the heavenly prize for which God, through Christ Jesus, is calling us.'

(Jeremiah 29:11; Philippians 3:13, 14, NLT.)

Afraid of fear

Being afraid of fear
Is what I am afraid of?
I am afraid.
Fear of living alone
Yet running away from people;
Fear of living
Yet I am medicated to keep me alive;
Fear of what people say
Yet they are already talking about me;
Fear of insomnia
Yet I have not slept for years;
Fear of self-harm
Yet my body has since been mapped by a
razor blade;
Fear of hallucinations
Yet I am always hallucinating;
Fear of getting lost
Yet my emotional compass is long lost;
Fear of being hit by a car
Yet I spend energy attempting suicide;

Fear of being an addict
Yet I drown myself in drugs daily.

I live in fear;
I am afraid of fear –
God, help me!

'May the LORD answer you when
you are in distress;
may the name of the God of Jacob
protect you. . . .
May he give you the desire of your heart
and make all your plans succeed.'

'Do not be anxious about anything, but in every situation, by prayer and petition, with thanksgiving, present your requests to God. And the peace of God, which transcends all understanding, will guard your hearts and your minds in Christ Jesus.'
(Psalm 20:1, 4; Philippians 4:6, 7, NIVUK.)

Who can save me?

Who can save me
From this heart of mine?
I struggle to know myself
Because I am never myself;
They say I should calm down –
How does it even feel?
I am using all my energy
To keep my head above the water.
What does it mean to be sane?
Fighting death
To stay alive
While others fight hard
To improve their flourishing lives.

They suggested therapy
But it left me reeling in pain.
They said exercises
But it left me
Seeing fellow athletes like ghosts.
They said social groups
But they left me with sounds
Echoing like a drum beat.
Can God save me?
Tell me! Assure me!

'Be good to me, God – and now!
I've run to you for dear life.
I'm hiding out under your wings
until the hurricane blows over.
I call out to High God,
the God who holds me together. . . .
God delivers generous love,
he makes good on his word.'

'O LORD, if you heal me, I will be truly healed;
if you save me, I will be truly saved.
My praises are for you alone!'
(Psalm 57:1-3, MSG; Jeremiah 17:14, NLT.)

Onlookers

They look at me
And they giggle,
Finding joy in my misery,
Calling me names
Because of my challenges.
They don't realise that
We both have battles;
It's only that mine are different from theirs.
Mine are visible for everyone to see –
They can see the scars;
They can see me being tearful;
They can witness my hallucinations –
But I am stronger than them
Because I have been fighting for years,
Battling for survival.
I am winning,
Because I am still alive.

'But he said to me, "My grace is sufficient for you, for my power is made perfect in weakness." Therefore I will boast all the more gladly about my weaknesses, so that Christ's power may rest on me. That is why, for Christ's sake, I delight in weaknesses, in insults, in hardships, in persecutions, in difficulties. For when I am weak, then I am strong.
(2 Corinthians 12:9, 10, NIVUK.)

'True wisdom is found in trusting God when
you can't figure things out.
He has chosen not to heal me,
but to hold me. The more intense the pain, the
closer His embrace.
Heartache forces us to embrace God out of
desperate, urgent need. God is never closer
than when your heart is aching.'
Joni Eareckson Tada

Through prayer and Bible study 'the mind of man is brought into communion with the mind of God, the finite with the Infinite. The effect of such communion on body and mind and soul is beyond estimate.'
Ellen G. White

'Never stop praying.'
(1 Thessalonians 5:17, NLT.)

'More things are wrought by prayer
Than this world dreams of.'
Alfred, Lord Tennyson

'You've kept track of my every toss and turn
through the sleepless nights,
Each tear entered in your ledger,
each ache written in your book.'
(Psalm 56:8, MSG.)

'We need never be ashamed of our tears.'
Charles Dickens

'The Lord *watches over all who love him. . . .'*

'So, humble yourselves under
God's strong hand, and in his own good time
he will lift you up. You can throw the whole
weight of your anxieties upon him,
for ***you are his personal concern****.'*
(Psalm 145:20, NIVUK;
1 Peter 5:6, 7, JBP, emphasis supplied.)

'I look up to the mountains;
does my strength come from mountains?
No, my strength comes from God,
who made heaven, and earth, and mountains.

He won't let you stumble,
your Guardian God won't fall asleep.
Not on your life! Israel's
Guardian will never doze or sleep.

God's your Guardian,
right at your side to protect you –
Shielding you from sunstroke,
sheltering you from moonstroke.

God guards you from every evil,
he guards your very life.
He guards you when you leave
and when you return,
he guards you now, he guards you always.'
(Psalm 121:1-8, MSG.)

'God whispers to us in our pleasures, speaks in our conscience, but shouts in our pains: it is His megaphone to rouse a deaf world.'

C. S. Lewis

'To all who are reaching out to feel the guiding hand of God, the moment of greatest discouragement is the time when divine help is nearest.'

Ellen G. White

'It is said that the darkest hour of the night comes just before the dawn.'

Thomas Fuller

'For He shall give His angels charge over you,
To keep you in all your ways.
In their hands they shall bear you up,
Lest you dash your foot against a stone. . . .
Because he has set his love upon Me,
therefore I will deliver him;
I will set him on high,
because he has known My name.
He shall call upon Me, and I will answer him;
I will be with him in trouble;
I will deliver him and honor him.
With long life I will satisfy him,
And show him My salvation.'
(Psalm 91:11, 12, 14-16, NKJV.)

'Child of My love,
fear not the unknown morrow,
Dread not the new demand life makes of thee;
Thy ignorance doth hold no cause for sorrow
Since what thou knowest not is known to Me.

'Thou canst not see today the hidden meaning
Of My command, but thou the light shall gain;

'Walk on in faith, upon My promise leaning,
And as thou goest all shall be made plain.

'One step thou seest – then go forward boldly,
One step is far enough for faith to see;
Take that, and thy next shall be told thee,
For step by step thy Lord is leading thee.'
Frank J. Exley

'Inch by inch, life's a cinch.
Yard by yard, life's hard.'
Author unknown

'Give your entire attention to what God is doing right now, and don't get worked up about what may or may not happen tomorrow. God will help you deal with whatever hard things come up when the time comes.'
(Matthew 6:34, MSG.)

Prayers

'Lord of great compassion, we pray You for those who are nervously ill, and too weak and anxious to lift themselves above the fear and sadness that threaten to overwhelm them. Do You Yourself, O Lord, lift them up and deliver them, as You delivered Your disciples in the storm at sea, strengthening their faith and banishing their fear. Amen.'

Elizabeth Goudge

'From chaos and emptiness,
From loneliness and lifelessness,
Come, Creator, come.

'From darkness and shapelessness,
From the abyss and awfulness,
Come, Creator, come.

'From fearfulness and hopelessness,
From weakness and dreadfulness,
Come, Creator, come.'
A Celtic Prayer – David Adam

'Father, we pray for the mentally ill, for all who are of a disturbed and troubled mind; be to them light in their darkness, their refuge and strength in time of fear. Give special skills and tender hearts to all who care for them, and show them how best to assist in Your work of healing through Jesus Christ our Lord. Amen.'

Timothy Dudley-Smith

'O God, the Creator and Father of all men, we praise You that Your will is life and health and strength. Help all who are ill or in pain to place themselves in Your hands in loving trust, so that Your healing life may flow into them to make them well and strong, able and ready to do Your holy will; through Him who has made known to us both Your love and Your will, even Jesus Christ our Lord. Amen.'

George Appleton

'Tender God,
Your gentle and kind-hearted love waits for us in the darkness and shields us from the light when it feels too overwhelming. We remember today all those who live in the depths of depression. Continue to cherish us all when we find it so difficult to cherish ourselves. Enable us to discover companions of compassion who will abide with us, as You abide in all things and in all places where the heart and mind aches for peace and a place of rest from the storm. We ask this in the name of our Brother and Friend, Jesus Christ. Amen.'

Christopher Newell

A blessing prayer

'May the Lord God bless you
each step of life's way.
May you learn each day to open yourself to
love and the blessings of love.
May you find a stick to lean on when the road
is hard – and not use the stick to beat
yourself. May you be blessed with life's
abundance and blessed in poor days too,
learning again what really matters, what lasts.
May you never give in to despair or the lie
that nothing can change.
May you find ways of life and walk them with
courage, knowing that every step is
within the heart of Christ, who holds all our
days in love.'

Reverend Dr Christopher Jenkins

'Hold me steady, Lord;
Let not winds or storms erode my roots.
Let me be strong, like an oak tree, tall and grace-filled,
Budding with expectant shoots.
Bending gently, through each season,
Waiting patiently for change.
Upright, righteous, full of life,
Giving shade and shelter with each bough,
Pushing roots so deep with growth,
Quenching thirst from eternal streams.
Hold me steady, Lord, strong and healthy;
Let my mind be close to Thee.'
www.lords-prayer-words.com

'Come and bring your hidden places;
Come and bring your hurting spaces;
Come and eat with hearts that break;
Come and drink, new worlds to make;
Come and feast, your vision spread;
Despair and Hope connect the fed.
Jesus says, "Come!" '
Christopher Newell

‘O Lord our God,
For those of us whose lives are strained and stressed . . .
Hear our prayer
and pour out Your peace.
For those of us whose hold on life is fragile . . .
Hear our prayer
and pour out Your peace.
For those of us whose illness makes them vulnerable . . .
Hear our prayer
and pour out Your peace.

'For those of us whose families struggle to
understand them . . .
Hear our prayer
and pour out Your peace.
For families and friends,
nurses, doctors and therapists
and all who seek to walk alongside
the stressed and strained, the vulnerable and
the fragile . . .
Hear our prayer
and pour out Your peace.
O Lord our God,
For all whose lives are in turmoil
through the effects of mental illness . . .
Hear our prayer
and pour out Your peace.
Amen.'
Mary Hawes

'God, help me to live a life for You. I long to be a whole person – consistent and united. Reach into my spirit and make me whole.'
Selwyn Hughes

'Beloved, I pray that all may go well with you and that you may be in good health, as it goes well with your soul.'
(3 John 1:2, ESVUK.)

'The eternal God is your refuge,
and his everlasting arms are under you.'
(Deuteronomy 33:27, NLT.)

End note

We hope you have found this little book helpful. The publishers strongly believe that trust in God is the ultimate solution to many of our problems, including anxiety and depression. In the same way, we believe He works through professional clinicians and counsellors, including their prescription medication. If reading this little book encourages you to exercise greater trust in God for healing, we applaud your faith. At the same time, we strongly recommend that you consult your medical doctor or health professional before changing any course of prescribed medication.